Sentimental Journal

For Audrey, Matthew and Jessica

I like to dance with the words as they flow
as we all become one and we search for our glow
Just spinning and soaring across the divide
then splash on the pages I've hidden inside

I like to play with the notes like a song
that make their own music while singing along
To find an escape from the traps that I hate
not get in the way of the things I create

Introduction

I wrote these poems myself... well kind of
some just write themselves but with
no witnesses I can easily take credit

There are 21 poems here from my
previous publications to share since
the other books are now out of print

There are also 34 new poems I have written
fairly recently and am excited to share!

Thanks so much for coming to visit

I hope you enjoy your stay

J.P. Gorham

Table of Contents

IF I EVER WALK WITHOUT YOU

If I ever walk without you
on a path beneath your cloud
I will listen for your whisper
from the outskirts of a crowd

Banished from the sense of touch
and blind I'll find the sound
Of where we met so long ago
and know you're still around

If I ever get too worried
that you didn't find your way
I will take a quiet moment
on my knees, and start to pray

An Angel down on Earth believed
eternity was here
So why would something sacred change
and love not still be near

If I ever take for granted
any portions of our time

Give a nudge, and then be patient
won't be long, or far to climb

The lessons we learned well enough
together seem to say
We know it's something special
when we treasure every day

If you ever walk without me
you will still feel my embrace
And my love will never leave you
or my smile, or my taste

So let's take these steps together
in the presence of the dawn
Like we'll always walk forever
even when forever's gone

SAVE A LITTLE MOMENT

Save a little moment
for some silence in your day
In twenty four short hours
every minute has its place

In the presence of a sunset
as the colors slowly fade
I can't think much of anything
to justify not staying

Save a place for someone
even if they don't show up
Always make more time for friends
than strangers making bucks

Let your life enjoy the flow
don't grab the horns too soon
And if you miss the sunset
watch the rising of the moon

No matter how you raise your kids
their life will still go on

And people who don't care as much
will be there when you're gone

So just make sure they get the love
and time and room to learn
You build up their foundation right
they'll get their rightful turn

Save an extra hour
for your children every day
I've had important meetings
that I've canceled just to play

But I have never been this rich
and hope the same for you
There's always time for sunsets
after all the work you do

FRIEND

As spoken tears are woven
through a single blade of grass
Just let me wipe away your fears
and show you how to laugh

When the past is left unclear
our instincts must prevail
Our tender spots through the years
will show us where we fail

But with a friend to share the pain
a new joy comes to be
For I have never been the same
since the day you came to me

So when you feel you can't go on
I'll carry you along again
Until once more we see the dawn
if just to let you know

I need you friend

Clouds before my eyes
gently wipe away my tears
And give me strength I've always had

to finally face my fears

JESUS (paraphrased)

A burglar made his way inside
a house with no one there
And started stuffing precious things
in sacks without a care

He looted through the jewelry box
took rings and watches too
Then headed to the living room
to see what he could do

He grabbed some speakers off a shelf
but then he heard a voice
"Jesus is here" he heard it say
he spun without a choice

He shined his flashlight all around
but finding no one there
He just unplugged the stereo
with expert, cunning flair

"Jesus is watching" he knew he heard
he spun around again

Determined now on seeking out
this new unwanted friend

He finally saw a parrot perched
as carefree as can be
"Who are you" he called out to
the feathered bag of fleas

"I'm Moses" was the birds reply
he almost laughed at that
And wondered if he had a friend
named Thomas the doubting cat

Or maybe there were snakes named Eve
and Adam in a cage
He shook his head at these new facts
and soon became enraged

Who would even name a bird
this "Moses" that you claim
It doesn't make much sense to me
I think you're playing a game

My name is true, was his response
the Bible was a source

For all my owner's animals
Mother Mary is their horse

The burglar stopped the bird right there
and said I understand
But this is sure unsettling
and it sure ain't what I planned

The parrot almost snickered then
and said I must confess
You sure won't like that Jesus
is our Doberman I guess

LADY

Lady, there's a sparkle
in your eyes and hair tonight
As I listen to the beauty
of the music you ignite

In my heart and in my senses
an explosion now erupts
As my spirit starts arising
like our souls are trying to touch

Lady, there's a magic
in your fingers and your voice
As your songs absorb my breathing
and I just don't have a choice

But to sit and wholly listen
to the holiness of you
That envelopes me completely
as it bonds me to your tune

Lady, I'm a liking
what I see and what I hear
From the inside working outwards
head to toe and ear to ear

It's a beauty never captured
by a camera or a pen
Makes me dream about the future
and I just can't wait till then

Lady, in your softness
and your outward inner strength
There's a time that can't be measured
by a volume or a length

For it's you who were created
to remind me why I'm here
So just keep singing sacred songs
and never disappear

TALL SHADOW ROAD (Ode to the Cavalry)

Somewhere down the highway
where the Aspens start to dwindle
are the remnants of our heroes who are owed

I have been there and I've seen it
on an unexpected turn off
to a place I learned to call tall shadow road

They were sometimes short in stature
but behind them is an outline
like a road map of their efforts still untold

They were humble, kind of quiet
yet inside them was a lion
who stands guard to watch their legacy unfold

There are many different sizes
though the shadows are all equal
and their saddles held them firmly as they rode

They would squint their eyes to focus
through the smoke of that injustice
even when a certain ending was forebode

See, there never was a blueprint
for the few who had the courage
when the face of death was added to their load

It is only in the nightmare
that should never be repeated
when the shells came down like hail to explode

They won't ever brag about it
but the truth remains for certain
that they never blinked and always lived the code

Some are living in our passions
some are somewhere in our teardrops
which is why they now reside where giants strode

If they ever had a chance to
they would change the circumstances
and wish everyone could stay in their abode

But they never even questioned
when their duty called them forward
and the need for them was greater and it showed

So I tell you now my Brothers
and my Sisters who will listen

when you pass the site that time has only slowed

You will see it if you're careful
to allow yourself the vision
and remember why our safety won't erode

To the soldiers who protected
where our freedom stands securely
I will take a quiet moment to unload

When my memories are passing
what so many just don't notice
I will tip my hat toward tall shadow road

MORNING

Billy woke up early
and poured himself some joe
He sat and started sipping
knew he soon would have to go

The cattle needed tending
'bout a dozen still were sick
And then he'd head out horseback
to that fence he had to fix

Well   he took another swallow
and the warmth offset the cold
It wasn't fear of freezing now
that made his leaving slow

It was how his life was changing
and how that made him feel
That stopped him for a moment
as he stared out to the field

See   his life's been mostly lonely
though he never did complain
He never stopped to wonder when
he'd come in from the rain

What was, just was, and wouldn't change
until its time had come
He couldn't hold the day just passed
or stop the rising sun

But that was then   and this is now
though both were meant to be
His smile just showed his preference
it was now that filled his needs

Upstairs   his wife was sleeping
with their baby by her side
and thinking of that picture
only filled his heart with pride

He finished off his coffee
took a final looking 'round
Then thanked the Lord for all he had
and left to tend the grounds

NEIGHBORHOODS CHANGE

I 'member long ago when time
was half a step to slow
And people stopped to figure out
just why you said hello

And every afternoon 'round three
you walked in through the door
That brought you cookies in the air
and knew what they were for

I 'member when we took our time
to get from place to place
And saw a lot of things we'd miss
when all we did was race

But racing had its time and place
And everything worked out
I miss those days with all my heart
and what they were about

I know that every neighborhood
is bound to have to change

I just lament how much the good
was lost to what remains

And though I can't return it back
to what it was before
I'll make the most of what it is
before it changes more

This world will keep on spinning
at the rate it always turned
No matter if we're fast or slow
and so I'm glad I learned

That even if the neighborhood
is changed it won't change me
You still can smell the cookies
when you visit me at three

JESSICA

One of Heaven's angels
found a way to leave the sky
And by some blessed miracle
you came into my life

and The joy helped me surrender
every fear I've faced before
Till hope and time together
let us find this open door

One of God's own children
came to touch a special place
That only tried to surface
when I saw your loving face

Only now can I be certain
there's a reason why I'm here
To help your growing taller
as you make my life so clear

My precious little daughter
when I brought you in this world

My life had something missing
till I saw my little girl

And your face made me remember
every sun I'd ever seen
Never shined on me as brightly
since I held my little queen

My brave and fragile lady
how can something start so small
And give me hope to strengthen
till I know we'll never fall

This life can be confusing
but together we'll be strong
I love you more than life itself
thank God you came along

PILLOW FIGHTS

She walked along and held her hand
a smile on her face
And thought about the night before
when she and Mommy played

The feathers flew around the room
with every contact made
Then giggles rose to fill the air
and out of breath they laid

They left the church and went outside
still blinking from the light
And watched the clouds that broke apart
and marveled at the sight

Then suddenly it came to her
she squealed in delight
Oh Mommy look the Angels too
have fun with pillow fights

THAT AWKWARD MOMENT

I wish that I was half the man
my puppy thinks of me
'Cause that's the kind of superhero
I truly want to be

I walk inside the door, he howls HELLO
I'm glad you're back
It's been forever you've been gone
your love is what I lack

I wish that every single person
felt this joy he shows
I walk a little further in
his excitement even grows

And even after saying goodbye
for hours as I left
He just wants more and more of it
the time we missed   A THEFT

Don't ever leave me here again
I just belong with you

I'm certain it was your mistake
oh... and sorry 'bout your shoe

My sudden guilt I can't express
with melting eyes on me
It's hard to say in doggy
"I came back to get my keys"

WISHING MOON

The sun's long gone, absorbed by night
the stars are laid out bare
The overwhelming darkness hides
the secrets they could share

The daytime critters snooze away
the nighttime shift now blinks
Just when it seems that time won't move
a moonbeam takes a drink

The rippled lake receives the light
and catches every bit
A single beam that pierced the might
exposes where I sit

I hear a fish release its bonds
then land in lunar glow
I see an owl's broad silhouette
enjoying the moonrise show

A whole new world now comes alive
the drama isn't missed
By those who simply took the time
to be celestial kissed

Now there are moments we should try
to make out fine details
But this is one to fade away
and let it fill your sails

I have a hope that you'll be here
when day digests the scene
To take us where the sunrise shows
the couple we should be

I see your face   and take your hand
faint flushing as I swoon
Watching you in mirrored glance
inside the wishing moon

MOTHER'S DAY

I haven't always been the friend
you stand before today
I've tripped and stumbled many times
from troubles in my way

But every time I felt alone
and needed someone there
You held me tight to let me know
how much you really care

I should have told you every day
but sometimes found it hard
And hoped you knew just how I felt
by looking in my heart

So just in case you still don't know
how much you helped me through
I send with all the love I have
these special words to you

THE SPECIAL PIG (paraphrased)

A travelling salesman made a stop
at Arnold Johnson's place
A few days after Christmas
when he saw a smiling face

He met the rancher   shook his hand
helped gather up some eggs
Until he saw a pig walk by
who had a wooden leg

He had to ask just how the pig
became a three-leg beast
There had to be a story
or a video at least

Well this here pig's a special one
came Johnson's quick reply
At night he sleeps inside the house
too good for any sty

It wasn't very long ago
our barn was full of smoke

And flames lashed out of every hole
this pig began to poke

Our sleeping heads until we moved
and finally awoke
Then ran off squealing to the barn
before the critters croaked

He got them out and lined them up
our family got out too
We looked at him with reverence
our grateful eyes just glued

So that was when he lost a leg?
the salesman inquired
Oh no   he didn't have a scratch
but he was surely tired

A little later Johnson said
I walked the woods out back
And didn't see it coming
when the grizzly bear attacked

That pig he came a running
As he dove right on that bear

Who ran off in the forest
like a demon sent him there

So that was when he lost his leg
the salesman insisted
Heck no, the pig was surely fine
his foot was barely twisted

Exactly one week later
my old tractor had a glitch
And rolled right back on top of me
and trapped me in a ditch

The water rose-up rapidly
my head was lowered quick
When I heard the splash of porcine
as he pulled his lifeguard trick

I lay there barely breathing
with a smile big and broad
The pig my superhero
his existence left me awed

I finally see the way your pig
has lost his little limb

It truly is a miracle
you lived because of him

But that's not how it happened
came old Johnson's final note
Our wonder pig escaped it all
and never even gloats

Then tell me what I'm missing here
the salesman retorted
The truth must be alluding me
the facts left misreported

I'm sorry if I mixed you up
don't feel like a dunce
A special pig like this you see
you don't eat all at once!

CHARLIE PARKHURST (A True Story)

Charlie Parkhurst drove a coach
as good as any 'round
And was tough as nails driven hard
in TO the sunbaked ground

Everyone would tell the tale
East West North and South
About the man who won the war
of battles of the mouth

Charlie used to hitch the team
as fast as lightning struck
Loading coaches quick and sure
he earned the greenhorn's trust

And moving out along the trail
he knew where things go wrong
He looked ahead   and all around
where trouble sang its song

Charlie Parkhurst spat and cursed
he never was polite
He never had to mince his words
or have to be well-liked

'Cause Charlie knew that etiquette
was good enough for church
But wouldn't save his leather hide
upon his driver's perch

Then came the day that Charlie died
his years of driving known
Many came to pay respects
and send his spirit home

The story told that sunny day
was heard all 'round the world
The toughest man to drive a coach
was actually a girl

So to those men who think that women
should only speak when asked
If Charlie were alive today
she'd have t' kick your butt

STARLIGHT

I'm not leaving you forever
I'm just warming up a star
I wish I didn't have to travel
but here I am and there you are

I don't blame this on misfortune
or being a human being with flesh
It's just that sometimes things can happen
when frozen stars and twilight mesh

I know you see me in the picture
ink stains bleeding from your tears
I try to tell you I'm here waiting
you tilt your head like you can hear

I swing my legs, then whistle softly
Für Elise for once in tune
I gave up everything that mattered
to take this trip beyond the moon

It isn't hell it's not quite Heaven
I guess it's somewhere in between

I fly around in tight spun circles
a patient man who's now unseen

I think of when we talked about it
a wrinkled smile on my face
I flick the frame that's on your dresser
it hits the ground to leave a trace

It must have been so hard to watch me
slowly fade by inch by inch
And I'm renewed but torn apart now
where every sound now makes you flinch

I don't know what's too familiar
I just know what's going on
I just came here to remind you
your star is warm and I'm not gone

DANCE IN THE RAIN

You don't have to wait
till storms are all done
To finally move on
or even have fun

It's not about finding
a place with no pain
It's all about learning
to dance in the rain

A new one approaching
will surely be so
So all of that waiting
will stop you from growth

Just face the raindrops
and wind with a smile
If needed, just fake it
to make the next mile

And slowly, but surely
you'll notice a change

That won't ever happen
 ignoring the pain

This might seem backwards
from what you defend
It's not what it costs you
but how much you spend

And what seemed expensive
will be the best deal
To get where you wanted
to help your heart heal

Try to be hopeful
and find your own style
Don't follow lemmings
who aren't worth your while

Always remember
the storms you've been through
Forgive the storm makers
if only for you

Leave a fair boundary
but never build walls

The lesson is balance
not having it all

Regrets can have reasons
so listen a bit
Sift through the chaff
in the place that you sit

Then get to your feet
and take the first steps
That's always the hardest
but it's all about reps

Your legs might seem wobbly
the rain might be cold
You might feel helpless
defeated and old

The wind might blow harder
the way steeper still
But soon you'll see mountains
have turned into hills

And what seemed to stop you
will be in the past

The thing about storms is
that none of them last

Don't carry anger

or think that you're done

I'll dance along with you

and head for the sun

DETOUR

Sitting on the side of a creek
near oak trees
Water still trickling
in summer retreat

Waiting for something
and tossing an acorn
Still sorting out
what I shouldn't repeat

Invisible monsters
and ghosts with a purpose
Clutter the pathways
defined by the fast

And so I deserted
the road with the street signs
Ending up creek side
absorbed by my past

The way that I've taken
was certainly useless

But I always tried
with a passionate heart

Delayed by the wreckage
concussioned by speed bumps
I witness the battles
that deepen my art

And so with a pen prick
that bleeds the page senseless
Arranged by the puddles
to question my fate

I'm finding the loss
of my sense of direction
In winds that keep swinging
a rusty old gate

ETERNAL

She spills out from my eyelids
makes a slow roll down my cheeks
She dances there beyond the mist
in memories that leak

I try to make her stay there
in the pastures of my mind
But gallop back on horseback
when the present's hard to find

She's more than I can handle
when I think I'm finally free
Like a spirit's constant vigil
spinning softly in the eaves

Without a conversation
as the words bring comfort home
To the sunlight left forever
in the place the shadows roam

I know I'll always love her
wish I held her in my arms
It's hard to lose the instinct
I should shelter her from harm

She floats just off the ceiling
when I lay in bed at night
Her lips still form a smile
when I come into her sight

We know the need to be there
but the truth just keeps apart
The power of the presence
that I hold inside my heart

A final new beginning
once again begins to fade
I fall asleep between the truth
and dreams this moment made

LADY MIST

She hovers o'er forests
where the sunlight starts to drift
In my eyes and through the treetops
where the chance of love is swift

And the dew that settled on her
made me feel like I've been kissed
Just so grateful for the vision
that we all call lady mist

And the shadows fall in fractures
like a million diamonds strewn
With her silhouette against me
as we fly across the moon

In the silence of the moment
every sense begins to twist
And I shudder in the presence
of the one called lady mist

Never sure of where we're going
I can feel the drops descend
Though I know the new beginning
I can never see the end

But it all just starts to mesh and
not a single thing is missed
I would trade all my forever's
for a dance with lady mist

So I leave you with a moral
and a story to be told
Of the days of countless minutes
through the path that will unfold

When I find myself in motion
I will grab it with my fist
Like I'll always live beyond me
in the arms of lady mist

CLOUD DANCING

To dance on the clouds
in dreams unaware

And make love as angels
on pillow-soft stairs

To run through the vastness
of small grains of sand

Is all I desire
when taking your hand

CATHEDRAL

The first scent of sage
still wet with its dew
The smell of old campfire
before it starts new

The coming of daybreak
still young in its growth
Are what hit my senses
my heart and mind both

The memories of stories
and poems we told
The stillness before me
that never gets old

This brief sudden moment
because I woke now
Is nothing but privilege
that I've been allowed

I look up to heaven
and say thank you Lord

For letting me witness
the things the night stored

Until it was proper
to stand and revere
The dawning of morning
that I witness here

Now back home it's Sunday
the folks dressing up
And fluffing their hair
and filling their cups

I've been there myself and
I've prayed in that church
But right now the prairie
demands where I search

The distant birds warning
the coming of day
That they're standing ready
and all's in its place

I drop to a knee
and lower my head

But keep my eyes open
absorbing this spread

And swear I've seen nothing
as pretty as this
Or listened so closely
and felt God's sweet kiss

Until I slept soundly
on just a thin cloth
Beneath this cathedral
He long ago bought

And so where we worship's
not what it's about
Or what congregation
though some have their doubts

But God only wants us
just where we belong
As long as we're praying
and singing His song

So dress mighty fancy
I'm sure He won't mind

Or ride on the prairie
with hands to the sky

Or simply adore Him
on vagabond knee
What's nice is the Savior's
not as picky as me

JUST ANOTHER POEM

It's just another poem
just a simple thought of mine
It's nothing that's too fancy
but it's clogging up my mind

I let the pen keep moving
till I purge the way I feel
It might not be impressive
but it sure as hell is real

It's just another ditty
like a doodle from my heart
Like I knew how it was ending
so I finally had to start

But it took another pathway
as I followed it along
And listened to the melody
till words became a song

It's just another poem
it will never change the world

It will never take for granted
my emotions as they whirl

If no one ever reads it
it was what I had to do
Remove the sudden roadblock
that restrained the path to you

It's just another passion
as it splatters on the page
And blasts the space around me
making words become the gauge

That tell me what I wanted
when I didn't have a clue
So I wrote another poem
for the love I have for you

CAMPING

The stars are my umbrella
As I sit outside this tent
The final log of wood
Has paid it's price and now is spent

I stir the glowing embers
with a stick that's laying around
Then watch a falling star
and make a wish without a sound

The chill of night engulfs me
but it's just not time to go
When galaxies are flying
up above and in my soul

There's something that I recognize
that took this trip to find
My eyes were shut wide open
when I leaned against my mind

I picture my life with her
then I think of being alone

I try to tell myself now
that I'll never find a home

But this moment tells me different
and my spirit never lies
Like a baby goes unnoticed
till it finally has to cry

So I'll just sit n' listen
to the angels from above
I reckon that I'm starting
to believe in finding love

A final subtle flicker
and the fire's finally gone
I've never felt this warm before
so far away from dawn

SWEET YESTERDAYS

My senses fill with wonder
every breath that I have left
As my memory still wanders
one more time put to the test

How once I saw my past before me
now it fades from view
I only wish that I had spent
my yesterdays with you

Tomorrow   if it comes as planned
I plan to be around
The tears that cry before me now
have softly changed their sound

Every movement that you make
I'll reach and meet with mine
And let you run so far away
as walking side by side

Somewhere in the inner depths
of dreams that came too soon

All of my sweet yesterdays
just seemed to bring me here to you

EQUINE FLIGHT

When I hug you from the saddle
feel and hear your heaving breaths
And the miles left behind us
were another simple test

Of the bond we have between us
that no storm or man can touch
I just tremble in the comfort
and your whinny says as much

The sweat stained smell of leather
and the wetness of your hair
Are a sweeter smell than flowers
as they dance into the air

With the prairie clouds descending
and the moonshine coming soon
In the sunset of emotion
every piece just joins the tune

When my song gets pretty tone deaf
and the harmonies collide

It's the closeness to the pavement
causing hope to just subside

A cappella just won't cut it
when compared to meadow flight
It's the duet of our chorus
that just makes the world feel right

Every note when doubled   triples
every bird upon the wing
Has a ballad I compare to
all the sacred songs we sing

Though this poem's short and simple
all the verses answer why
Your four legs   my out stretched wingtips
winds from Heaven   make us fly

DRIVER

I used to drive a coach here
'bout 20 years ago
I used to love to ride the wind
and let them ponies go

My years may be a dwindling
but I've got no regrets
I used to be the best there was
and that I can't forget

Now some of my old cronies
they just sit around a jug
And if they weren't so dang burned mean
them boys could use a hug

Their tears just drown their whiskey
though their sorrow makes some sense
I'm about to join them there
up on the pity fence

see When I was just a youngin'
I lived out on a ranch
And though I weren't but three feet tall
at least I had my chance

I'd chase off all the chickens
and gather up their eggs
Then run 'em to my Mama
fast as wind I'd move my legs

And when we'd take the wagon
gather sticks to start the stove
My Pa knew where the best ones were
down by the old Oak grove

Each year I just got bigger
got to do a little more
And step by step my folks would give me
slightly tougher chores

Till one day I was driving
and I got my first small taste
Of moving with a team that flew
as wind and hair whipped face

I knew THEN what I was born for
I could feel it in my bones
Oh I just kept a learning
'cause I knew I'd found my home

And when I reached the birthday
of my 22nd fall
I wired old Wells Fargo
told them all about my call

It said I know you're happy
with the drivers that you got
But you ain't seen the likes of me
and I deserve a shot

I've been driving since I breastfed
held a rein before I crawled
And I'm as tough as nails boys
I've never even bawled

And there's never been a horse alive
who's half as smart as me
Well then again   there was ONE once
but I was only three

Now I know I oversold it
but I HAD to drive a team
And when their answer came back quick
I thought it was a dream

It said "You sure have brashness
and that's what we're trying to find
If you're a man who don't touch drink
you're just the perfect kind

The'll be a few weeks training
and we'll have to size you up
If you're as good as all you bragged
we'll wean you from a pup"

Well my folks were sad and happy
didn't want to see me go
But somewhere there behind their fears
his pride, and her love showed

And with a final hug goodbye
I turned to face my fate
And took a final breath inside
and crossed the cattle grate

Though I was going somewhere
I was always meant to be
My folks though trying to smile through tears
made parting bittersweet

I made it into Frisco
and I learned all that I could
Then before I even knew it
I was driving like I should

For years I followed trails
some, I'd never seen before
But always brought them folks back home
and left to pick up more

And I never took for granted
what my peers would sometimes call
The toughest job in all the West
I always had a ball

But then one day my bosses
came to Big Nose Kate's saloon
And said we need some talking
and they took me in a room

They told me they were grateful
for the job that I had done
But I was getting old now
they need room for someone young

Now if I were more insightful
I would swear they'd thought I'd cry
But I just thanked them for my years
shook hands   and said goodbye

See I've always done the best I could
and worked with what I had
As happy gathering eggs for Ma
as chopping wood with Dad

And only by enjoying
every chance that came my way
Was how I learned to let it go
when progress led to change

And so I might not handle
the ribbons like I did
But I can still work twice as hard
as when I was a kid

And every sun that rises
I will greet with open arms
Appreciate what I still have
old age ain't done no harm

And if my friends would listen
I'd say   at least you drove
You had a chance that so few had
and you just whine and moan

No, you won't catch me crying
for what ain't here no more
Complaining 'bout them better days
or feeling mighty sore

'Cause every day I wake up
I thank the Lord who gave
Another chance to rise and see
I'm still not in my grave

CROWN KING GLADIATORS (with Chris B)

There's a fire on the mountain
burning like a crown of thorns
The folks and wildlife passing
as the heroes rush the storm

The smoke as thick as river fog
below the birds of prey
Coyotes start their howling
like they're praying for monsoon rain

A homeless mountain lion
keeps on searching for its mate
The fire burns too hot   too fast
we hope it's not too late

Tarantulas and Rattlesnakes
just hide and start to stare
As people make a foreign world
in the distant town of Mayer

The many times we've witnessed
plumes of smoke, and checked the wind

Still never could prepare us
for the nightmare that begins

The frantic planes and choppers
racing daylight and terrain
Keep on shifting where they focus
'cause it never stays the same

I guess we shouldn't build our homes
where fire's meant to burn
But that's just where the beauty lies
it has to have its turn

It's sad to lose a box we love
but it really just is stuff
So as we pray no humans pass
we accept that that's enough

Life is all a balance here
for good as well as bad
And sometimes it's not 'til it's gone
to find just what we had

The flames that now destroy here
are the only way to start

The ancient holy cycle
that is etched on nature's heart

Rebirth and renewal
are the great creator's plan
Like a Phoenix from the ashes
blades of grass grow where we stand

And that supports the flowers
stops the rain from running down
So like a brand new sunrise
we will all rebuild this town

It only takes a pile of sticks
to make a brand new hut
But this will still be sacred ground
when eyes return to shut

19 RAYS FROM HEAVEN

19 rays from Heaven
reach down through Prescott skies
Embrace and then encircle us
as if they heard our cries

Our hearts are clearly shattered here
these sons our sole concern
We know we'll never be the same
and struggle where to turn

19 of our finest men
who spared us from demise
On Yarnell hill, to save the town
swung strong with hero's eyes

A final man on lookout calls
it's time to turn and run
He did his job while Angels wept
and took our 19 sons

19 lives of valor live
through roots grown wide and deep

Their family and friends of friends
is where their love will sleep

We just don't want to listen 'cause
it's still too soon   too raw
In time it might just make some sense
but know just what we saw

These 19 rays have touched us
as we've felt them seep inside
Their hands upon our shoulders when
a thousand stood and cried

We see it in the spirit
as we circle 'round their kin
So even as we mourn our loss
we know that God will win

The 19 rays embrace us
and we hug their families tight
They hold their hurting babies
who will face another night

With their Daddy, Son or Brother
in another lonesome place

The only way that we'll pull through
is in those 19 rays...

I've fallen onto bended knee
let dirt turn mud with tears
I know their souls are still alive
where time is free from years

But in this heartbreak moment
all I wish that I could do
Is turn back time, but these are thoughts
that's left with me and you

GRANDMA'S ATTIC

Up in Grandma's attic
where we used to hide away
Exploring nooks and crannies
we could lose ourselves all day

There were secret hidden treasures
full of castoffs from the past
We would daydream of our Grandma
with the special things we had

In a trunk   a world was opened
faded pictures spoke of times
When the world was somehow simpler
and it seemed to come alive

So then we'd play for hours
never bored and eyes wide bright
Didn't matter where we turned around
we'd see a different sight

Every corner filled with what nots
giant nets, and fishing poles

Nuts and bolts and tools that Grandpa
used to build the house we know

And like a jigsaw puzzle
piece by piece it made more sense
That who we were was just a part
of past and present tense

On rainy days we'd sneak away
to where we felt so safe
We'd try on clothes that made us laugh
and think of what has changed

And winter nights at Christmas time
we'd stay up there on cots
And as we slowly fell asleep
Grandma filled our thoughts

SNOW KISSED

The world pulls up its blanket
as the snow begins to fall
I watch with eyes wide open
at the wonder of it all

The birds start their migration
heading South against the winds
The leaves all here have fallen
as the winter now begins

I pull my jacket tighter
pull my gloves up on my hands
Then head on down the trail
where the wilderness demands

That I marvel at the picture
and I soon become as one
With the changing of the seasons
and the fading of the sun

The earth is slowly covered
with the whiteness of the times

As I write another poem
of the scenery that rhymes

It has a natural flowing
that begins to write itself
But I could never capture
what I witness by myself

I take my pen and paper
then I put them on the ground
I take a deeper breath now
as I listen to the sound

Of everything together
in a symphony of light
My poem   still unfinished
only pales before this sight

HERO

Let me tell you of a hero
who's the bravest soul I know
She is scared and she is shaking
but she faces every foe

With a soft determination
never followed in a crowd
Even when she mumbles whispers
hope and joyful are allowed

Let me tell you of an idol
I could only dream to be
And the ever-growing outlook
that she always will believe

It is so much more courageous
to be scared as hell and try
Than be the ones who mock with
scorn and envy in their eye

Let me tell you of a lady
so much taller than she thinks

How her world is still evolving
with emotion as she blinks

She is frightened   she is fearless
she is passion pushing through
And has learned from being unwoven
to untwist a cynic's view

Let me tell you of a friendship
that survived and sought to grow
Like a teammate fighting demons
back to back with swinging blows

For it never gets too easy
but I dive back in the water
With a new-found love for swimming
just so proud that she's my Daughter

LITTLE THINGS

I care about the smaller things
that most just pass right by
The kid that's trying to find his place
with tear drops in his eye

I care about forgotten ones
at Father/Son events
And those who need their Mama still
and what their absence meant

I care about the underdog
who has a heart of gold
Especially when they shiver
in the outside where it's cold

I care about the challenges
that unsuspecting folks
Will have to know when staggered
at the butt of bully's jokes

I care about the single Moms
who have to work so hard

They often just forget themselves
and have to stay on guard

I care about the elderly
society forgets
When changes in the fabric torn
leave constant growing debts

I care about neglected pets
who never have a chance
When shiny flashy puppies trapped
in pet store windows dance

I care about the little guy
the ladies left with doubts
The person who still tries so hard
when rumors force them out

I care about the veterans
as right and left just whine
I wish that I could push them to
the front of every line

I care about the struggling girls
and what they have to face

The Dad in me just wishes he
could hug them back in place

I care about the fortunes lost
when greedy people lie
I'd change it all for certain
if I had the chance to try

I care I never hardened
in the tragedies I've known
And understand the way it feels
when left out on your own

I care enough to change myself
and where I've fallen short
So I can fully know the path
to give a fair report

I care enough to sit a spell
and listen to the hearts
Who only waited for the chance
to let their dreaming start

I care and I'm so grateful
for an ever loving God

Who cares enough to change me
in the toughest times   I'm awed

I care about the left behind
and how they question why
It breaks my heart in pieces but
I'm not afraid to try

IN MY SILENT NIGHT

In my silent night
I know I'm just a man
Trying to be a better one
each day I get to stand

To face a new reminder
displayed in splattered speech
That scatter to the corners where
they never leave my reach

In my silent night
adjusting to this place
The less I talk the closer
angel faces bring their grace

To where they solemn vow
my kiss at breath of dawn
Waken with wide-open eyes
to show the fear is gone

In my silent night
a thousand stars collide

But never touch the passing one
that soon becomes my guide

The splendor of the moment
that's bringing me a peace
And only what the storm has left
allows its calm release

In my silent night
this Christmas hush allows
A scent of ginger snaps the air
and mingles with the boughs

Green and glow and tinsel
dance there on shadowed wall
Until we're just intrinsic
with the spirit of it all

In my silent night
as pale moon descends
Approaching on the darkness where
it tries to make amends

And learn the reason laughter
is curing all my ills

To share with me this meeting
of our minds and hearts and wills

In my silent night
as a melody is played
With soundless virtuosity
of love that God displayed

And if you really listen
you will hear the silence sigh
A brief relief of confidence
that mingles with the sky

In my silent night
as holy words just come
Whispers from another world
that beat a primal drum

And hum until I'm hearing
from the awesome voice of Christ
Fall below like virgin snow
that hope and prayers enticed

In my silent night
I bow, and praise the Lord

For letting even fools like me
learn reasons He adored

And loved us all as equals
no matter who we are
I close my eyes and smile here
beneath my Christmas star

MOMENTS ALONE (my first poem)

My dreams are still the same
only tears could change the scene
My yearnings still are calling
for another chance to be

I lean against a memory
and let the sea pass by
And feel the drops fall off my cheeks
but I can't seem to cry

The moment that I let you go
just slowly drifts away
I watch you from a distance
as we both live different days

And see beyond your eyelids
where my mind has never known
But for now I'll watch the ocean
from a moment left alone

LAUGHTER ON THE WAY (To Michael)

Another moment falls exposed
to struggle with the pain
A life believed now takes its toll
but still my love remains

Another feeling in the wind
we follow to our souls
Then close our eyes to leave us blind
and let our dreams unfold

We've stood together hand in hand
faint teardrops in our smiles
And stopped to wonder why we're here
still running all the while

We've cried alone throughout the years
just strangled by our thoughts
And slowly found each other
when the whole world seemed so lost

But lessons learned don't always stay
the way they came to be

We all need time to live it out
to see what we can see

The endless arm we reach with care
still burning from the flame
I wrap with all the love we've shared
and laughter on the way

HARVEST MOON (free verse)

a harvest moon hangs low
enveloping weariness...

igniting with passion

the spark

that lifts
and incorporates me

winking it's playful eye
as gravity
dissolves

I watch in weightlessness

my ties loosened
reminded suddenly
(with urgency removed)

to breath...

if only for a moment

release obstructions
of Earthly bonds

and float...
gently

twisting away...

HIGH VALLEY RANCH (To Doug and Greg)

He made his last trail ride
cross a meadow of green
Stopped and thought for a moment
with his heart caught between

Then a slow moving tear drop
gently rolled down his face
Said a prayer for his loved ones
made a sigh full of grace

He's too young to seek Heaven
but too old for this Earth
He was sorry his Mother
who had witnessed his birth

Said goodbye to his body
but his spirit remains
In the wind that just whispers
as it crosses the plains

For a moment he cried out
If I could, I would stay

But he heard the Lord calling
as the world fell away

It was time, and he knew it
blew a kiss   held his breath
With a final conviction
full of courage met his death

And his friends felt the sadness
and his family knew
We were all a lot smaller
when we found out the truth

But he's riding on trails now
on a horse that just floats
Through a forest of glory
hearing Angel touched notes

It's the song of the passion
and the chorus of life
That we just can't imagine
left alone in this strife

But don't think for a moment
that a tragedy struck

Or the short time he lived here
just ran out of luck

For he lived a full lifetime
it was just planned that way
In the womb, Jesus knew this
and he came to the day

When the struggles just vanished
and eternity called
And he made the last passage
sending love to us all

Don't waste precious daylight
for our days are so few
It's so easy to wander
like we all tend to do

But we all have a purpose
if we listen then act
On the blueprint provided
for the Lord has our back

We will ride on the trails
that are lined with the clouds

When we finish our journey
that creation allowed

But it's time to start climbing
till we reach the last branch
As we start to prepare
for the High Valley Ranch...

MOMENTS IN YOUR LIFETIME

There are moments in your lifetime
that just stop you in your tracks
When you know you'll never be the same
and won't be going back

I've learned so many times before
I'll never learn it all
From time to time however
life just serves a wakeup call

There are moments in your lifetime
when you have to stop and see
That the universe is bigger now
with billions of dreams

But kids who sit in front of me
with smiles and mile-wide eyes
Remind me what it's all about
and humbles me inside

A child with stage 3 cancer comes
and takes me by the hand
As another with leukemia
is moved to finally stand

And then one more who shows me
how we all are truly blessed
There is nothing but this moment
and this moment is the best

I came to hopefully remind
these kids that life is joy
No matter what our challenge is
for every and girl and boy

We only have the fleeting day
it's all we really have
But learned that what they have to give
was more than what I had

This world is filled with scared adults
who run to lead the way

And stop at certain mountain tops
exhaustion on display

There's also many petty folks
who threaten day to day
When witnessing the happiness
that stands before their way

But the wisest individuals
I've had the chance to meet
Are 16 children losing hair
who won't accept defeat

There's no worries what tomorrow brings
no danger in the fact
That strangers with their smiley eyes
might never make it back

For it's all about the friendships here
and moments they were made
No matter where our paths will wind
these precious thoughts won't fade

And the only thing that's permanent
is the fact that life will change
It's how the big adventure here
brings wonder to the day

And when it all was said and done
and chaff was free from grain
I found that there were four main points
of why I really came

To listen to the smallest child
ignore life's push and shove
It is joy   it is hope   it is faith   it is love
and the greatest of these is the love

GRATEFUL

I'm grateful for the friends who stayed
and those who walked away
It's always on the stormy seas
where sailor's skills are made

I'm grateful for my failing health
that showed me more to life
And made me look much further
at the reason for the strife

I'm grateful that the liars proved
the price that truth has paid
I watch their 15 minutes peak
then smile as they fade

I'm grateful in a quiet thought
that God is always there
Who let this year be what it was
made sure that I still care

I'm grateful for the reset switch
but glad it won't delete

The lessons that I learned to date
and never will repeat

I'm grateful that the cruelty shown
made me a better man
I cherish my compassion more
I'm proud of where I stand

I'm hopeful that I'll get a chance
when waking up each day
To breathe the beauty in the air
entwined I'll dance and play

I'm grateful that I fully know
this day might be my last
So I embrace and truly thank
my splendid, ugly past...

PASSAGES (for Coco and Noel)

I can feel the mist drenching me
but the pain goes far deeper
So I pay it no mind

It was only yesterday
I held you in my arms
How it seems so long ago

Houselights are coming on
one by one
Across the lake now

Streetlights are slowly flickering out
as I jump my last fence

I wake with a shudder
as light breaks through my dream
I know I know the truth
but still I grab and dial the phone

A thousand rings each one a pin
that pierces through with ease

I never thought I'd ever
find myself back here alone

A far off cry in answer
only witnesses the change
I have to wonder where it goes
and why it ever came

A turn to face the sunrise
comes to meet another day
But the glass slips from my fingers
and the shards imbed their trace

Through stages undistinguished
and a scattering of will
I begin another journey
will it take me further still

I try to read the morning news
but all it has to say
Is that she died, with phone in hand
and crying her boyfriend's name

NIGHTMARE (For Coco and Noel)

It's been a good long time now
since I let myself just cry
It's not that I'm that hardened
there just wasn't reason why

I understand perspective
with the crap that I've been through
But this here is a moment
I just quiver in my boots

It's never more than Jesus
ever knows that I can take
But feel right now His trust in me
might be a big mistake

I guess I have to man up
push myself a little more
And make it to her funeral
that tears me to my core

They say that I'm a hero
but there's things they surely miss
When I know that I'm a failure
'cause I'd kill to feel her kiss

As the rock in my foundation
only trembles like a quake

You can give me hope tomorrow
but for now just let me shake

For I never thought a sunrise
ever came without her face
And I know I have to hold on
to her memory and grace

I will do the task that's needed
but I'll always feel her near
I can't stop the storm that's breaking
and I'll have to face my fears

It's been a good long time now
since I held her long ago
And I never can replace her
but I just can't let it show

That I hold her in my pillow
as I soak it to the bone
That I've never felt so naked
so exposed and so alone

I will get up put my boots on
first the left and then the right
Then I'll grab my hat and head out
if I make it through the night

But for now, the endless darkness
doesn't seem to have an end

As I fall back down in terror
that my heart will never mend

But I know I wouldn't trade this
for a life we never met
I will always count the blessings
and I never will forget

In the lost and quiet moments
she will still be here to see
That I'll feel her arms embrace me
even when I'm on my knees

And I know she'd never want me
to be void of any hope
So her spirit right beside me
has to be enough to cope

With her pure and precious lessons
on a pedestal and perch
In the morning as I'm sobbing
I will head off to that church

SEQUEL RAIN

tiny drops
of how she felt
explode, and greet
a changing world

the fear returns
as candles melt
I wake again
without a girl

why she hides
is why I'm missing
crying inside
to hope concealed

twisting
shaking
reminiscing
burning   in this distant field

TALKING TO ANGELS

I'm sitting by the creek side here
as water ripples by
And watch a brook trout leaping
for a most delicious fly

A lesser goldfinch stops and peeps
at mule deer having lunch
The tender reeds are such a treat
they smile with every crunch

I start to rise as thunder clouds
move in to let me know
That nothing ever stays the same
so we should let it flow

The mountains rumble casually
debate my deep concern
Then monsoon drops remind me
that we always need to learn

In rain with no umbrella
as a figure comes in view

Delights my awkward senses
and I know just what to do

I see my Nana, take her hand
in whispers I confess
I'm seeking heaven more and more
this world I'm liking less

We walk along the creek bank
never struggling for our words
Or worrying where the time will go
embracing what we heard

For hours days weeks and months
with nothing left to prove
The second hand upon my watch
has hardly even moved

I hug my Nana, kiss her cheek
and look into her eyes
The face I see reflected there
has no fear of goodbyes

It never seems uncomfortable
or strange when she returns

I'm talking to the Angels who
have come to take their turn

I'm waiting on a park bench
for the visit to begin
My girlfriend comes up strolling
like a welcome summer wind

I then complete a sentence
that I started long ago
It's not "'til death" that we will part
there's so much left to know

She looks at me and crinkles
up her eyes to drink me in
The vision only quenches
where my thirst betrays my skin

I wish that I could follow her
when clouds seek her return
But here I stay to finish up
as distant fires burn

The first dear pony that I rode
was Candy such a love

But nothing can surprise me
when she lands from up above

She drops her head invites me
as I climb up on her back
And like we've done in vivid dreams
we fly off down the track

The pure communication
that we first learned here on earth
It doesn't even miss a beat
reminds me what I'm worth

Whoever thought that angels
had to be the human kind
Has never known the love we share
or why we stay entwined

My favorite canine Ziggy
runs with Mischief his best friend
They leap into the air and land
in arms they quickly mend

There isn't time for worry
every moment is a treat

We wrestle till the daylight fades
and know this ride is sweet

We all should talk to angels
when we find it's tough to climb
And wish that we could be one too
but not before our time

But if we only listen
to the things that we can see
We hurt ourselves and those we love
and never are complete

Visit hours must be done
For I stand here alone
I ponder for a moment why
I'm left here on my own

But only find acceptance
to prepare myself for more
After talking to the Angels
who have walked this way before

ARIZONA

When I was only 12 years old
I climbed aboard a Greyhound bus
And headed where the sunset rose
towards the Arizona dust

And somewhere East of Kingman
where Saguaros made their stand
It came to me that this was where
I'd learn to be a man

The cactus turned to Chaparral
then slowly into pines
The yellow dirt was soon blood red
the higher that we climbed

The purple yellow orange
in the broad stroke painted skies
Took my spirit like a river
as it filled my awestruck eyes

From Williams to Flagstaff
south to Prescott mile high

Through Dewey-Humboldt up the road
from sweet Sedona skies

With copper whispers in Jerome
I felt like something changed
I grew as fast as Phoenix has
and never was the same

Several weeks just passed right by
and soon I headed home
A boy was taken from the land
and sent back on his own

But Arizona stayed with me
and knew that I'd return
A childhood-touched epiphany
I'm blessed I got to learn

COMMON STORMS

Get your nose above the cloud line
fight like hell to make it so
Let the lessons of the battle
keep the raging storm below

There are thermals there is soaring
this is struggling for your soul
But conditions get much softer
when your spirit takes control

In your mind a wheel's turning
as a rusty music plays
Loosened dust from ancient harp strings
turns the air a brownish haze

That just spins around in circles
with your doors and windows closed
I have followed those escape plans
and it left my fear exposed

When I aimed my wings to heaven
I had wounds from being shot

I had promised not to give up
even though I did a lot

But the place of twisted normal
is a line I won't re-cross
With the strength that I can muster
I will stay above the loss

Where the warmth of silent sunrays
slowly melt a thousand deaths
That are right below the cloud line
as I listen for your breaths

From that flight we all make solo
with encapsulated view
As you aim above the thunder
where I float and wait for you

UGLY (U Gotta Love Yourself ~ Inspired by Anita B)

I have a little statue
on a string around my neck
It's name is just plain "UGLY"
but it saves me in a wreck

As it soaks in jagged edges
that I brush against each day
But then at night I take it off
and wash that pain away

It's not a superstition
or diversions that I paint
It's just a soft reminder
that was witnessed by a saint

To try to pay attention
to the sorrow and the strife
Then wipe it clean to help each day
find balance in my life

We never need a necklace
if we use it like a crutch

But sometimes just a simple tool
can really change so much

So if I'm truly careful
not to wallow but to grow
I find that it's the surest way
to let my ugly go

I hope I'm not the reason
any ugliness ensues
But if I am I'll start to scrub
the black that brought those blues

There's somewhere many sorrys
just become revolving doors
Till rolling sleeves and scrubbing
is the only cure for sores

So don't ignore the ugly
it can fester it can hurt
Or accelerate the winter
till the snow just drowns the dirt

For all of us have ugly
but we ALL have beauty too

It just depends on what we wash
when darkness clouds the view

The seeds we plant will grow here
if the thaw in spring is slow
There's just no point to speed it up
or challenges won't show

The real point to "UGLY"
is the beauty that I find
When fingers on this necklace
meet my soapy water mind

COMING HOME (Recovery Poem)

Don't forget the tenderness
you learned to hide so well
The softness of your sweet compassion
taken by this hell

Let your heart remember thoughts
that used to help you through
And as your raindrops start to fall
just know I think of you

The pain of transformation stabs
and tears the flesh from bone
It bites and stings and rips and jabs
and leaves you on your own

But if you face just why you're scared
allowing fear to move
You'll learn to finally recognize
It's here to heal and soothe

Rivers come from streams that came
from springs that hid their truth

And springs are pools of drops of rain
that started in your youth

And pain you felt and carried through
from clouds that held those drops
Began the never ending chain
of heartache change and loss

The foothill paths you followed then
to find the waters source
Have now come back to where and when
your life gets back on course

So lightly step and feel your way
and know you're not alone
There's nothing sweeter in this world
than finally coming home

THANK YOU

Thank you sweet Jesus
for saving my soul
I don't deserve it
but You brought me home

The world almost crushed me
and left me to die
But You raised it off me
I still don't know why

Thank you sweet Jesus
for teaching me faith
And showing me gently
that You are the way

I crawled with the beggars
the place I belonged
You lifted my vision
to sing this new song

Thank you sweet Jesus
for giving me hope
Your endless forgiveness
has helped me to cope

And now that I'm finding
my life is raised higher
It's from Your example
that I can inspire

Thank you sweet Jesus
for showing through me
That You are the answer
and chose me to be

The broken clay vessel
once left by the road
That's now filled with water
and kept overflowed

JUDGMENT (paraphrased)

A farmer had to go to town
one early Sunday morn
So he prepared his finest clothes
fresh pressed and barely torn

He laid them out and went to bed
as Saturday resigned
Figuring he'd go to church
before he got supplies

He slept so deep he barely dreamt
and woke by break of dawn
He saddled up his pony fast
and soon they both were gone

It'd been a while since he'd been there
he marveled at the change
The little church had been torn down
a mansion in its place

He tied his horse and went inside
and found a quiet seat
And looked straight up and all around
this place was quite a feat

The folks they started settling down
and soon a man appeared
He started with some fancy words
 of fierceness, hell and fear

But then he stopped and saw the man
who'd ridden many miles
He shook his head as he approached
the farmer full of smiles

The preacher thought he'd make a point
and had the man stand up
Then pointed out his ragged clothes
compared an empty cup

He told the farmer he should leave
and go back home to pray
And ask the Lord what he should wear
when he was in God's place

It shows a lack of true respect
continuing his rant
I'm sorry but it just won't do
to wear your working pants

The farmer simply chose to go
and mounted up his ride

He stopped outside the general store
to gather his supplies

He rode the lonely path to home
and thought about those words
Deciding not to figure out
the message that he heard

But late that night when he got home
he kneeled down to pray
And right away he heard a voice
that took his breath away

He said a quiet thank you Lord
and settled for the night
The peace he felt gave restful sleep
he rose with dawn's new light

All week long he carried on
content to do his chores
A grateful man for what he had
he didn't need no more

Then suddenly came Saturday
he pressed his clothes again
And said his prayers and went to bed
and fell asleep by ten

Before the light he woke and rose
and saddled up his horse
He didn't need to get supplies
but God has planned his course

He passed the dancing meadow grass
he passed the aspen trees
He passed the hawks that circled high
he passed the swollen streams

He passed the flowers framing rocks
he passed the passing deer
He never took for granted once
the reason they were here

And finally he got to town
and found himself a seat
The mansion didn't quite impress
as much as what he'd seen

He didn't hardly notice heads
that turned towards his place
He smiled and waited patiently
with silent humble grace

The preacher rose to start again
then stopped right in his tracks

He asked the farmer there and then
why he still wore his sacks

The farmer softly just replied
Well, I told God your concern
And asked him what I need to wear
when next week I return

The Lord He answered right away
His point was quickly done
How would I know what to wear
I've never been there son

MATTHEW

I never stop myself enough
to smell the fragrant rose
And often never take the time
to watch it as it grows

I've seen enough to know that life
will never go as planned
But as I grow with passing time
I start to understand

This life can be confusing
from its first day to its last
And many puzzles never solved
will stay there with the past

But this I know and share with you
my Son as life begins
Success is a direction
not a race you finally win

Though many try to take their share
when it's not found with ease

And sometimes it's so hard to care
when watching from your knees

You have to love the trials too
or you won't truly find
The love that God has given you
to rest your weary mind

So take the time and smell the rose
I'll lift your face to see
The beauty that is left exposed
though I can't make you dream

But there is something I can give
which came from God above
The only thing that can't be changed
the promise of my love

SONG OF MYSELF

There was a time
when my mind couldn't rhyme
And my thoughts had no place to be

But there in my mind
I knew it was time
To learn the song of myself

There was a moment
like all passing hopes
That I found it was more than it seems

And there in the moment
I thought I had lost
I know it was always with me

Is it a pastime
or a glimpse of the future
To smile in the face of despair

When all thoughts are pain
and life's not the same
Somehow I find I still care

Well life can't get harder
nothing's left here to lose
But at least I've still got my own help

So I swallow my pride
and laugh deep inside
And keep singing the song of myself

There was a thought
still unknown I found
That brought me where I can't believe

Confusion of reason
or change before growth
But there I was down on my knees

There was a time
when the world didn't rhyme
But to some it was something to see

Well now it's all mine
if I just take my time
And know that it's everyone's dream

Does it seem now tomorrow
is still hard to find

A place, you need all the while

Does it feel like the past
has left you behind
But somehow you still need to smile

Well life could get harder
than it already is
Not everything's taken away

So I feel like I do
cause this far I've got through
And the song of myself's not afraid

TRY

Try to look at life the way that God does
the bluest marble set against the sky
Try to understand just why it glistens
and know it's not a sin to wonder why

Try to make mistakes that only dwindle
always try to beat the time before
God will give the answers if you let Him
a simple faith that helps you to explore

Try to look at Earth like we're in training
a temporary place to lay your head
Look around at all that just surrounds you
to live each day like it's your last instead

Try to be forgiving those who shame you
but never let them tell you who you are
When it all is said and done won't matter
when you and God are hanging on a star

Try to look at life the way that God does
just living for forever when you do

God is so much more than just a legend
and all He has is lasting love for you

Try to move on forward through the darkness
keep on trying until you touch the sky
Never give up trying to keep on trying
until you know the how and when and why

Be your best but never think you're better
all are equal the day that they arrived
Inch by inch just work to keep on crawling
until your shaky legs show you survived

Try to look at life the way that God does
much bigger than the steps beneath your feet
Having all the tools you need to get there
will show you how to overcome defeat

WHY WE DANCE

We dance because the mountains move
beneath our nimble feet
We dance until the spirits sing
and beg we keep the beat

We dance to show we just can't live
without the joy of life
We dance or we would simply wilt
if we can't dance tonight

We dance to prove our value's
so much more than what we own
We dance in sacred circles
in a group or all alone

We dance to call the nourishment
that brings the food we need
We dance to keep sustaining
when the rain has reached the seed

We dance to meet our longing
far away from where we are

e dance to hold it closer
as we weave the earth and stars

We dance inside our bodies
to release another world
We dance and see our failures
healing slowly as we whirl

We dance outside the hardships
so the work will still get done
We dance around the fire
when it's hard to find the sun

We dance along the chasm
till the emptiness is free
We dance with blessed knowledge
every moment has to be

WHEN THE RIDING'S DONE

You know I'll always ride here
even when my riding's done
In the whisper of the pre-dawn
or the final burst of sun

At the corners of transition
where the changes are obscured
I will ride and if you see me
it's because our love endured

You know I'll never leave you
even when I'm far away
In the moments when the words stop
and your breath gets in the way

I will softly say I love you
barely louder than the breeze
So I hope you gently listen
to my voice between the trees

You know I'll try to hold you
even when my arms can't grasp

Just to try to bring you comfort
when your throat lets out a gasp

The feelings that we share here
will transcend just what we see
And my horse will still be waiting
right beneath our favorite tree

You know we are forever
but it's easy when we're here
Just a hand away from holding
and a hug away from fear

But you have to make a promise
that your hope will never run
And you know I'll always ride here
even when my riding's done

SOLITUDE

As sunrise hits the mountain
and the glisten starts to gleam
And the patches slowly melting
make their way toward the stream

Where the deer herd drinks in safety
when coyotes go to bed
There is just a spark of joyful
in my eyes and in my head

In the cities and where townsfolk
like to gossip to their friends
Where the people stand in contrast
to the facts their message sends

I will visit with a smile
I will mean the hands I shake
But when sunset hits the treetops
then my heart will start to ache

For my quiet time with nature
and the way it all just works

When no outside interventions
take away the natural perks

It is all about a balance
and bombardment needs a break
But it's just about impossible
to worry on a lake

I gave up processed animals
and what's not cared about
But all I want for breakfast
is a big fat rainbow trout

A tug upon my bobber
starts another moment awed
The only place I want to be
is placed this close to God

The
End